Original title:
When Love Hurts

Copyright © 2024 Swan Charm
All rights reserved.

Author: Olivia Orav
ISBN HARDBACK: 978-9916-79-170-7
ISBN PAPERBACK: 978-9916-79-171-4
ISBN EBOOK: 978-9916-79-172-1

Fables of the Disenchanted Heart

In shadows deep, where whispers dwell,
The heart once bright now bears a shell.
Yet even dim, it seeks the spark,
For hope shall rise from darkest dark.

In prayerful sighs, the soul does weep,
For lost tomorrows, dreams to keep.
Yet grace alights on weary brow,
To guide the heart to know the how.

Through trials faced, the spirit bends,
Each stumble teaches, every end.
In pain, the truth begins to show,
A path to peace where love can grow.

For fables told of hearts that break,
Bear witness to the risks we take.
In every scar, a tale unfolds,
Of faith renewed through love that holds.

So lift your gaze beyond the night,
Embrace the dawn, the purest light.
For in the fables intertwined,
The disenchanted heart shall find.

In the Shadow of Grace

In the hush of twilight's kiss,
We find a gentle light,
A whisper born of holiness,
Guiding hearts through night.

In the shadows, faith shall stand,
A beacon shining bright,
With every prayer, a tender hand,
Leading souls to right.

Beneath the stars, we seek our place,
In silent reverie,
Embraced within the arms of grace,
In sweet humility.

Oft we wander, lost in dreams,
Yet love will find a way,
In the quiet, hope redeems,
A promise for the day.

As dawn breaks forth, a sacred sound,
A chorus soft and pure,
In the shadow, joy is found,
Our hearts forever sure.

Echoes of a Silent Benediction

In the stillness of the heart,
A prayer without a voice,
Echoes linger, souls impart,
In solemn, quiet choice.

Benedictions softly fall,
Like petals from the tree,
Absorbed within the sacred call,
In timeless unity.

Each heartbeat is a whispered grace,
In silence deeply known,
Finding refuge in this space,
Where love and peace have grown.

The world can fade, its clamor cease,
Here, in the heart's embrace,
We cultivate a sacred peace,
In every sacred trace.

The stars above may fade from view,
Yet light remains within,
For every silence births anew,
A chance for hearts to win.

Sacred Mourning

In the shadows of our grief,
We gather hand in hand,
With hopes that time can bring relief,
And heal us as we stand.

In sacred space, we share the tears,
In love's embrace, we dwell,
Remembering those lost through years,
In stories we can tell.

Each whisper carries on the breeze,
A name we hold so dear,
In memories, our hearts find ease,
In echoes, they are near.

Though sorrow weighs upon our souls,
We lift our prayers above,
In mourning's truth, our spirit rolls,
To find the light of love.

So let us gather, hearts unite,
In honor of their grace,
For in their absence, still shines bright,
The love we can't erase.

The Parable of Unrequited Yearning

In the valley of desire,
Where shadows weave and blend,
A heart ignites a sacred fire,
In hopes that love will mend.

Yet longing stretches like the sky,
A vast, unyielding space,
With every tear, and every sigh,
An ever-distant face.

Wisdom whispers through the night,
In every silent prayer,
That love will blossom, take its flight,
Beyond the weight of care.

Though unreturned, the heart remains,
A vessel of pure grace,
Each yearning, woven in our veins,
A testament to faith's embrace.

In shadows deep, we learn anew,
That love's a sacred quest,
For in the yearning, we pursue,
A path toward the blessed.

Hymns of Hallowed Heartbreak

In shadows deep, we softly tread,
Where echoes of the past are spread.
A heart once whole now torn apart,
Yet still we sing with hallowed heart.

With every note, a prayer we lift,
A melody of love's lost gift.
In darkness, faith will be our guide,
Through every tear, our souls abide.

The wounds we bear, a sacred trust,
In loss, we find our path to dust.
Each heartbreak whispers tender grace,
In sorrow's arms, we find our place.

Though time may heal, the scars remain,
In quiet moments, there's sweet pain.
Yet hymns of love will never cease,
In brokenness, we seek our peace.

So let the music gently flow,
In every heart, the seed will grow.
For in our grief, we shall impart,
Eternal hymns from hallowed heart.

The Confession of a Broken Promise

In whispered vows, we once believed,
Yet time and doubt, our faith deceived.
The words I spoke now haunt my nights,
A promise lost, in shadowed lights.

I sought your hand through trials faced,
Yet lingered doubts I had embraced.
Forgive me, Lord, for paths I chose,
In fleeting moments, my faith froze.

The altar stands, a witness still,
To dreams I shattered, broken will.
Each tear a testament I bear,
In silent prayer, I lift my care.

Redemption calls upon the breeze,
With humble heart, I drop to knees.
Though trust was lost, I seek the way,
To mend the bonds that went astray.

With every breath, I'll strive to be,
A faithful heart in humility.
For in the silence, hope restores,
The promise kept forever endures.

Grieving in Sacred Spaces

In sacred spaces, hearts embrace,
Where sorrow dwells, and pain finds grace.
Beneath the stars, with gentle whisper,
We mourn the past, love's tender crisper.

The candle's flame flickers in prayer,
For all the souls, lost unaware.
We gather close, in unity's bind,
In grieving hearts, our hope we find.

Each tear that falls becomes a prayer,
A sacred act, a love laid bare.
In silence, memories softly flow,
In sacred spaces, seeds will grow.

With every breath, we honor strife,
In grief, we touch the pulse of life.
Through loss, we find a deeper truth,
In sacred spaces, reclaim our youth.

So let us walk with heads held high,
In sorrow's arms, our spirits sigh.
For in this journey, love's embrace,
We heal our wounds in sacred space.

Redemption in Tears

In every tear, a story told,
Of battles fought, and hearts consoled.
With every drop, redemption calls,
In sorrow's depth, our spirit falls.

Yet through the pain, a light breaks through,
A promise made, forever new.
For tears like rivers cleanse the soul,
In sacred flows, we find our whole.

In moments dark, we find our strength,
Through trials faced, we go the length.
Each tear, a seed of hope reborn,
In brokenness, our hearts have worn.

The journey vast, the path unclear,
Yet faith will guide us, ever near.
A dance of joy amidst the plight,
Through every tear, we find the light.

So lift your heart and let it bleed,
In sorrow's grace, we plant the seed.
For in the depths, redemption lies,
In tears of faith, our spirit flies.

The Trials of a Celestial Love

In the heavens high above,
Where whispers dwell in light,
Two souls are bound by faith,
In shadows, they fight the night.

With each tear, a lesson learned,
Through trials, love finds its way,
Beneath the watchful stars,
They rise with the break of day.

Their hearts aflame with passion's grace,
Yet humbled by the trials faced,
In every struggle, they grow strong,
A bond that nothing can erase.

Amongst the echoes of the past,
They seek the promise of a dawn,
Their spirits dance in endless skies,
Together, forever drawn.

Thus, through trials, love will soar,
Eternal as the shining sun,
For in the depths of their despair,
They find the light, and both are one.

Meditations on the Edge of Despair

In the stillness of the night,
Where shadows softly creep,
Thoughts entwined in solemn prayer,
As the weary close their sleep.

A heart abandoned in the dark,
Casts dreams upon the wall,
Each whispered plea a dagger's bite,
In anguish, I can hear the call.

Yet in the depths, a flicker glows,
A flame that flickers bright,
For hope shall rise from ashes grey,
To lead me back to light.

Amidst the pain, a gentle hand,
Caresses my restless soul,
With every tear, a story unfolds,
In the chaos, I am whole.

So here I stand, on edges frail,
And in the silence, I find grace,
From despair's edge, I leap in faith,
To find my sacred place.

The Ritual of Goodbye

In the hush of fading light,
Two hearts prepare to part,
With whispered words of sorrow,
they seal the bond that's heart.

A ritual of tender grace,
With every tear that falls,
The memories woven tightly,
In love's bittersweet calls.

Each gesture speaks the heart's intent,
A silent vow to treasure,
Though distance stretches far and wide,
Their moments are a measure.

So in this sacred space they tread,
With reverence for the bond,
Embracing all the love they've known,
Vowing to carry on.

And as they drift on separate winds,
Their spirits intertwine,
In every breath, a prayer ascends,
Forevermore, they shine.

Sanctuary of the Desolate Heart

In the quiet of my solitude,
Where shadows softly weep,
I build a sanctuary,
In a heart that's worn, not weak.

Walls of faith enclose me tight,
With echoes of the past,
I gather all my shattered dreams,
The lessons learned, steadfast.

Each crack within the surface glows,
A testament of grace,
In every struggle, light shall spring,
To guide me through this space.

The stillness whispers softly here,
Embracing every pain,
In this refuge, I find strength,
The heart can bloom again.

So in the desolation's arms,
I seek the light anew,
For in the depths of solitude,
The love of life breaks through.

Litany of Love's Misfortunes

In shadows deep, the heart does tread,
With every vow, a prayer unsaid.
The winds of chance, they call our name,
Yet love remains a fleeting flame.

We held the stars, both bright and rare,
Yet found ourselves in vacant air.
The tears that fall, a silent song,
In love's embrace, we felt so wrong.

Each promise made was like the dew,
That formed and vanished, lost from view.
We chased the light, but left the dark,
In every ache, a shattered spark.

Companions once on paths we roamed,
Now glance at echoes where love's combed.
Yet from the pain blooms wisdom's grace,
In heartache's wake, we find our place.

For in the end, though love may yield,
Each bruise we bear, a truth revealed.
In shadows cast, we learn to see,
The light within, our souls set free.

A Covenant of Empty Promises

In quiet whispers, vows entwined,
A sacred pact, yet hearts resigned.
What once was gold, now turns to dust,
In love's great scheme, we place our trust.

By candlelight, the words were spun,
To chase the dark and greet the sun.
Yet time has shown a fractured thread,
For every word, a tear instead.

We promised worlds, a realm so bright,
Yet linger now in endless night.
The tapestry of dreams once whole,
Now frayed by years, has lost its goal.

With every tear, a bitter space,
Where hope once thrived, now leaves no trace.
An empty throne where love should reign,
Echoes of joy, now bound in pain.

So here we stand, two souls at bay,
In silence cruel, we drift away.
Yet in this void, we seek the dawn,
To mend the rift and carry on.

Blessings Woven with Heartstrings

In gentle threads, our lives entwine,
Each heartbeat sings, a sacred line.
The blessings shared, both near and far,
In love's embrace, we raise a star.

When joy and sorrow dance as one,
We find our peace beneath the sun.
The laughter shared, the tears that flow,
Are vibrant hues in love's tableau.

Through trials faced, we forge our flame,
In every rise, we bear love's name.
These heartstrings strummed, a melody,
Resounding softly, setting free.

For moments brief, yet oh so dear,
Create a bond that conquers fear.
Each gaze the spark, each touch divine,
In love's own light, our spirits shine.

So let us weave with tender grace,
A tapestry that time can't erase.
In blessings told, our hearts we share,
A journey paved through love and care.

Altered States of Grace

In prayerful breaths, we seek the light,
Transcending woes, embracing night.
Each whispered thought, a silent plea,
To find the truth that sets us free.

In altered states, where spirit roams,
We wander far from earthly homes.
The sacred dance of soul and time,
Repent and rise, like verses rhyme.

With every fall, a lesson learned,
In grace we grow, and hearts are turned.
The clouds may darken, storms may roar,
Yet in our depths, we find much more.

In moments small, the world awakens,
The path of love, though strewn with shakin'.
From ashes drawn, new light can shine,
In every fracture, a grand design.

So let us trust in fate's embrace,
This sacred journey, filled with grace.
In altered states, we'll rise as one,
With hope anew, our hearts can run.

The Epiphany of a Desolate Heart

In shadows deep, my soul has cried,
Yet in the night, Your light abides.
Whispers of grace, in silence flow,
Awakening hope, as darkness slows.

A barren field, where dreams once bloomed,
I wander lost, in paths entombed.
Yet through the haze, a truth appears,
Your love transcends my darkest fears.

With every tear, a seed I'd sow,
Through pain I learn, through loss I grow.
You lift me up, when I am frail,
In Your embrace, I'll not derail.

The desolation, yet I'm alive,
A spark ignites, my spirit thrives.
From ashes rise, a heart renewed,
In faith, I find my solitude.

So in this desolate, sacred space,
I seek Your truth, I seek Your grace.
In every sigh, a prayer I send,
Your love, my strength, my hope, my friend.

Beneath the Cross of Unfulfilled Promises

Beneath the weight of every vow,
I stand in grief, I ponder how.
The burden stings, unspoken fears,
Yet faith persists beyond the tears.

Each promise made, now draped in loss,
I find my solace at the cross.
With heavy heart, I cry to Thee,
Unravel all the mystery.

The echoes of what might have been,
In shadows long, my thoughts begin.
Yet still I yearn for grace to bloom,
Transcending deep, despairing gloom.

The light breaks forth, a gentle ray,
Illuminates the darker way.
Beneath the cross, I lay my shame,
In hope to rise, to live, reclaim.

For every dream that turned to dust,
I place my faith, Lord, in Your trust.
Though unfulfilled, these paths I roam,
In love's embrace, I find my home.

The Theology of Loss

In every tear, a lesson learned,
Through every heartache, wisdom earned.
Loss at the altar, faith laid bare,
Yet in the void, Your love is there.

The world spins on, with fleeting time,
Yet through the struggle, hearts can climb.
Awash in grief, a sacred thread,
A tapestry of souls long fled.

Embrace of sorrow, bittersweet,
Unfolds the beauty in defeat.
For in the aching, we must know,
Your grace sustains, Your mercy flows.

Though shadows loom, the spirit soars,
Through pain we learn, through love restores.
The theology of loss, a creed,
In every wound, a promise freed.

So let the fire of faith ignite,
Transcend the trials, embrace the night.
For loss unveils the hidden gain,
In brokenness, we live again.

The Liturgy of Lingering Goodbyes

In whispered tones, the farewells sound,
A liturgy where grace is found.
Every heartbeat, a sacred sigh,
In moments shared, we dare to fly.

With heavy hearts, we tread the line,
Memory's glow, a gentle sign.
In every glance, a world resides,
A tapestry of life that hides.

Yet in the parting, love remains,
A sacred bond that never wanes.
Though paths diverge and silence reigns,
In spirit's echo, joy sustains.

The weight of leaving lingers still,
Yet through the ache, we find our will.
With prayers unspoken, hands once clasped,
Eternity's promise, forever grasped.

So let our hearts, in faith unite,
Beyond the shadows, into light.
The liturgy of goodbyes endured,
In every loss, love reassured.

The Echoing Rites of Heartache

In silence, shadows whisper still,
The heart beats soft, against its will.
Lost dreams linger in the air,
An echo lingers everywhere.

In prayer, we seek the light to find,
Yearning souls, forever entwined.
Each tear released, a sacred rite,
A journey through the endless night.

With faith, we gather every shard,
In brokenness, our spirits guard.
A sacred bond, though stretched and torn,
In heartache's arms, we are reborn.

Together still, we walk this path,
Consolation in the aftermath.
Each step a vow, we tread with grace,
In seeking peace, we find our place.

The echoes fade, but love remains,
In brokenness, we bear our chains.
Yet in the depths of sorrow's song,
We find the strength to carry on.

The Reckoning of Fractured Devotion

Upon the altar of trust we stand,
With trembling hearts and open hands.
Each promise made a fragile thread,
Through trials faced, our spirits bled.

In shadows cast by former grace,
We search for light, a warm embrace.
To reckon all that once held truth,
In fractured dreams, we seek our youth.

Each moment shared, a bittersweet,
In loving still, we taste defeat.
Yet through the cracks, a glimpse of light,
Awakens hope in darkest night.

Our hearts laid bare, we rise anew,
In every wound, a path runs true.
The reckoning of love unfolds,
In sacred tales forever told.

Together, though we've lost our way,
In fractured devotion, we shall stay.
With every trial, our bond will grow,
In love's embrace, we'll find our glow.

Virtues in the Wake of Absence

In absence, virtues take their flight,
A tapestry of day and night.
For every echo of a sigh,
Each memory whispers, 'Why not try?'

The heart remembers every glance,
In shadows deep, we find our chance.
With open arms, we learn to hold,
The lessons wrought in silence bold.

Forgiveness blossoms in the air,
A gentle balm, a soothing prayer.
Though miles apart, our spirits twine,
In absence felt, our love aligns.

Courage rises in the strong,
It guides the weary when they long.
Through trials faced, and bridges burned,
The flame of hope forever yearned.

In virtues found, our souls unite,
Though absence weighs like endless night.
With faith to guide, we'll journey on,
In every heart, the dawn will dawn.

The Eulogy of Our Unwritten Chapters

In pages blank, the stories wait,
The future calls, beyond the gate.
With every breath, a tale unfolds,
In every soul, a truth beholds.

We weave our dreams in silent nights,
Through whispered prayers, in shining lights.
Each moment shared, a fleeting breath,
Yet in the silence, we find depth.

The eulogy of paths untraveled,
In hopes and fears, our hearts unraveled.
Each choice we make, a gift bestowed,
In love's embrace, our spirits glowed.

Though chapters pause, the story flows,
In every heart, a wisdom grows.
The unwritten lines, a canvas vast,
In timeless grace, our shadows cast.

With faith, we pen the words to come,
In eulogies of love, we become.
Together still, we chase the dawn,
In every ending, a new song.

A Shrine of Shattered Hearts

In shadows deep where silence calls,
A shrine of tears, the heart enthralls.
The echoes of a love once bright,
Now whisper soft in endless night.

Each prayer a sigh, each hope a ghost,
For every soul that mourns the lost.
Yet still we seek, though broken part,
A flicker of light to mend the heart.

The cobblestones bear witness still,
To every ache, to every thrill.
In sacred space where spirits weep,
The promise of healing, a bond to keep.

Hold tight the shards, embrace the pain,
For in the hurt, we rise again.
A tapestry of human plight,
We weave our sorrows into the light.

Together we stand, hand in hand,
In this shrine, united we band.
For love endures, though hearts may break,
In shattered pieces, we still partake.

Through Pearls of Pain

Through pearls of pain, the soul must tread,
In trials faced, by faith we're led.
Each drop a lesson, each ache a guide,
In darkness deep, the light resides.

The burdens borne, a heavy load,
Yet on this path, our spirit grows.
From anguish springs a well of grace,
A stronger heart in each embrace.

With fervent prayers, our voices rise,
To seek redemption in the skies.
In every tear, divine design,
A sacred truth, a love divine.

In quiet moments, solace finds,
The broken hearts, the weary minds.
Through pain we forge the bonds of kin,
In every ending, anew begin.

So let us walk, though paths may bend,
In unity, our spirits mend.
For through the storms, we'll surely gain,
The beauty born through pearls of pain.

The Silent Benediction

In silence lies a sacred hymn,
A benediction soft and dim.
The whispers of the heart's request,
In quietude, we find our rest.

With bowed heads, we seek the way,
In stillness, every truth will stay.
Each moment cherished, every breath,
A testament to life, and death.

The stars above, they shine with grace,
Illuminating the holy space.
In reverence for the paths we tread,
The silent words of love unsaid.

Among the leaves, the shadows dance,
An invitation to the trance.
Embrace the peace that softly flows,
The silent love that always knows.

In every sigh, a prayer unfolds,
A gentle warmth that never grows cold.
Within the heart, a light we hold,
The silent benediction, pure as gold.

A Covenant of Sorrows

In shadows cast by ancient trees,
We gather here upon our knees.
A covenant of sorrows made,
In every loss, a bond displayed.

With every tear, the heart attunes,
A symphony of grief that prunes.
Yet in the depths, a promise glows,
The seeds of joy that life bestows.

Through trials fierce, our spirits soar,
In steadfast love, we find the core.
Together strong, we bear the weight,
A tapestry of fate we create.

Each whispered prayer, a lifeline drawn,
In unity, we greet the dawn.
For every wound that time bestows,
A healing grace that softly flows.

So hand in hand, through dark and light,
We bind our hearts, a sacred rite.
In love we trust, as sorrows part,
A covenant grown in every heart.

Divinity in Despair

In shadows deep, I search for light,
A whisper soft, in the still of night.
The faith I hold, though worn and frayed,
Confirms the promise that's gently laid.

Through trials fierce, my spirit bends,
Yet in the storm, His love transcends.
For even when the path is steep,
The heart remembers, the soul can leap.

With every tear, a prayer I send,
In sorrow's clutch, my soul to mend.
In darkest times, divine does weave,
A tapestry of hope to believe.

So when despair's cold veil is cast,
I lift my gaze, to Him steadfast.
For in the night, the stars do shine,
A testament of love divine.

The Altar of Sacrifice

At dawn's first light, I kneel in prayer,
My heart laid bare, my burdens share.
On sacrifice, my faith relies,
In each lost hope, a strength that flies.

The altar stands, both worn and true,
Where love is shed, and old made new.
In every loss, a gain I find,
For in His pain, my heart aligned.

With open hands, I give my all,
Amidst the rise and the weary fall.
For in surrender, grace will flow,
And from the ashes, blessings grow.

In every tear, a lesson dear,
Through every trial, He draws near.
A holy gift, this path I tread,
To find in loss, what love has bred.

Silent Prayers for a Shattered Soul

In stillness found, a cry unheard,
Beneath the weight, I seek His word.
A shattered heart, yet whole I feel,
For silent prayers, the soul can heal.

In quietude, the spirit stirs,
A gentle nudge, where hope accrues.
Each moment beckons, a chance to rise,
To lift the veil and seek the skies.

With every breath, a trust implied,
In shadows dim, my faith abides.
The pain I bear, a sacred quest,
Leads me to Him, my soul's sweet rest.

For every wound, a story told,
In fragile grace, I find the bold.
Thus, through the storm, I learn to dance,
In silent prayers, I find my chance.

The Crossroads of Heartache

At twilight's bridge, I stand alone,
A weary heart, a weight I've known.
With choices made, yet dreams betrayed,
I seek the path where hope has laid.

In crossroads faced, the fork appears,
With whispered truths, a voice that cheers.
For in the pain, new roads can shine,
To lead a heart to love divine.

With each step forward, courage grows,
Amongst the hurt, His wisdom flows.
In shattered dreams, a vision clear,
A light will spark, dispelling fear.

So here I stand, with heart in hand,
Transformed by grace, at love's command.
Though heartache waits, I choose the fight,
For in the dark, He brings the light.

A Covenant Frayed by Time

In the twilight of our days, we stand,
Promises whisper as grains of sand.
Fading echoes of vows once made,
A threadbare bond in twilight's shade.

With every tick, the clock reminds,
Of sacred oaths that fate unwinds.
Heaven weeps in silent grace,
The tapestry unwoven, lost in space.

Yet hope lingers like morning dew,
Reviving faith in hearts so true.
Can we mend what fate has torn,
And find new light in love reborn?

Through trials faced and burdens shared,
A flicker remains where we both cared.
The covenant may fray and fray,
But in our souls, it finds a way.

For though the years may dry the ink,
In love's embrace, we find the link.
And in this frayed yet sacred thread,
The spirit lives where angels tread.

Chasing Shadows of the Divine

Beneath a sky of endless night,
We wander in search of a guiding light.
With every step, our hearts ignite,
Chasing shadows, we yearn for sight.

The stars above, they play their game,
Unraveling secrets, whispering names.
In the silence, we hear the call,
A sacred dance in the dark's thrall.

Each moment a prayer, each breath a plea,
To glimpse the face of divinity.
Through valleys deep and mountains high,
Our souls ascend, reaching the sky.

In the stillness, we find our way,
Through wandering thoughts that guide the day.
With faith as our compass, we shall seek,
The heart of God, tender yet meek.

And though the path may twist and turn,
In every shadow, our spirits yearn.
For every fleeting, sacred sign,
We find ourselves in the divine.

The Sacrament of Farewell

At the altar of parting, we stand tall,
With heavy hearts, we hear the call.
In sorrow's depth, we find the grace,
As memories linger, time can't erase.

Each tear we shed, a story told,
Of love that blossomed, of hands we hold.
The sacrament binds us with gentle ties,
Though distance stretches, our spirit flies.

In farewells whispered beneath the stars,
We cherish the moments that healed our scars.
With every hug, a silent prayer,
A promise sealed in the open air.

As seasons change and paths diverge,
In the quiet, our souls emerge.
With faith, we step to what's unknown,
For love's true bond can never be overthrown.

So let us part with grateful hearts,
For every ending, a brand-new start.
In the echoes of goodbyes well spent,
We find the blessing in the sacrament.

A Pilgrimage of Longing

In the hush of dawn, we set our quest,
To seek the sacred, our spirits blessed.
With weary feet on ancient ground,
In every step, our hope is found.

We walk through valleys, climb steep hills,
With each breath drawn, our faith instills.
In every shadow, a promise gleams,
A pilgrimage born of sacred dreams.

Through bustling towns and quiet streams,
The heartache whispers, the journey redeems.
With open hands and weary hearts,
We gather wisdom as the world imparts.

Beneath the stars, our prayers arise,
Every longing echoing in the skies.
For what we seek is not far away,
It dwells within, illuminating the day.

As we traverse this winding road,
We seek the light, share every load.
In longing's embrace, we find our way,
A pilgrimage of love that won't decay.

The Cost of Unspoken Affection

In silence dwells a heavy cost,
The words unsaid, forever lost.
Hearts tremble in the muted night,
Yearning for a touch of light.

Promises linger in the air,
Hopes wrapped in a cloak of care.
Yet fear hushed each tender sigh,
As moments flicker, passing by.

The weight of love, a sacred chain,
Bound in joy, yet steeped in pain.
Fractured dreams, a whispered plea,
Longing for what cannot be.

Let not the heart in shadows roam,
For silence builds a hollow home.
Speak, dear soul, and let love soar,
For in the word, there's so much more.

Forgive the cost of words unsaid,
Find solace where your heart has led.
Embrace the truth that love demands,
And gently clasp those unseen hands.

Intercession for a Weary Heart

O heavy soul, take pause and pray,
A balm for trials faced each day.
In whispered hopes, find strength anew,
In silent grace, all burdens too.

The weary heart in shadows lies,
Where daylight dims and sorrow sighs.
Yet through the night, a star shall gleam,
A promise bright, a hopeful dream.

Lift up your eyes, embrace the dawn,
For in each tear, love's light is drawn.
With every breath, let faith unfurl,
To guide you through this troubled world.

A prayer ascends, a gentle plea,
For peace to reign, for hearts to free.
The weary find their solace here,
In love's embrace, cast off all fear.

Let kindness flow like rivers wide,
Refresh the soul, be love's true guide.
In intercession, hearts find grace,
And weary souls, a resting place.

Saints of Solitude

In quiet corners, spirits dwell,
The saints of solitude, they tell.
With faith embraced in whispered prayer,
They dance with shadows, light the air.

Each moment still, a sacred space,
Where broken hearts can find their grace.
In solitude, a lesson learned,
To seek the light and be returned.

The echoed sighs of dreams untold,
In silence, warmth of love enfold.
The sacred bond of one alone,
Can find the truth that shines like stone.

Revered in silence, wisdom grows,
The saints who walk where stillness flows.
Each thought a prayer, each breath a song,
In solitude, the spirit strong.

Let not the world dissuade your heart,
For in alone, we play our part.
The saints of solitude arise,
In quiet light, their virtue lies.

The Gospels of Dissonant Love

In tangled paths where lovers roam,
The gospels speak of hearts unhome.
With every note of broken song,
A tale unfolds, where love feels wrong.

What sacred text could hold the strife,
Of love entwined with bits of life?
For in the clash of joy and pain,
A deeper truth, we can't restrain.

The echoes of dissent be loud,
Yet in the rift, our hearts are bowed.
With bruised embrace, we learn to see,
That love can thrive in harmony.

The dissonance, a thread divine,
Weaving through moments, intertwine.
And in the grief, the laughter sighs,
For love endures, it never dies.

Through scripture torn, our spirits soar,
Embracing all with open door.
The gospels sing of every hue,
In love's discord, we find what's true.

The Divine Downfall

In shadows cast by heavenly light,
The mighty dwell in doubts of night.
Their crowns of gold turn cold with rust,
In the silence, they lose their trust.

The whispers soft, like autumn leaves,
A warning note that no one heeds.
Once so proud, now broken clay,
In the end, all must bow and pray.

The stars above begin to fade,
Forgotten hymns in darkness laid.
The world a tapestry unwound,
In humility, true grace is found.

From ashes rise the meek and mild,
With open hearts, like a tender child.
For in the falls, the spirit soars,
Embracing flaws, we open doors.

Divine descent leads souls anew,
In every heart, a light shines through.
For as we crumble, seeds are sown,
In brokenness, we find our home.

Surrender at the Feet of Pain

At the altar of anguish, we find our way,
With heavy hearts, fragility on display.
Each tear a prayer whispered low,
In surrender, our spirits glow.

The burden felt, like thorns entwined,
Yet grace is found, in pain aligned.
We bow our heads, our will now released,
In this brokenness, we are increased.

Through trials fierce, the soul laid bare,
In the fire's embrace, we learn to care.
Each scar a story, a testament true,
For in our wounds, love breaks through.

Let go the fears, let faith arise,
In surrender, our spirits fly.
At the feet of pain, we humbly kneel,
And in that ache, our hearts can heal.

In darkest nights, the dawn shall break,
With every doubt, new strength we make.
For pain is but a merciful guide,
Leading us to the light inside.

A Testament of Lost Reveries

Once dreams danced like shadows bright,
Now echoes drift in endless night.
A testament to what we've lost,
In every wish, we count the cost.

The sunlit paths now cloaked in gray,
Where laughter lived has slipped away.
Yet in the ruins, hope may bloom,
Through silent sorrows, love finds room.

A flicker of faith, a whispered prayer,
In shattered moments, we find our care.
For every loss a seed is sown,
In falling down, we find our throne.

The past may haunt, yet guides our feet,
Through shadows deep, the light we greet.
With every tear, new strength we gain,
In every heartbeat, we break the chain.

So hold the memories tenderly near,
For in their midst, God's voice we hear.
A testament of dreams that fade,
In our hearts, they're lovingly laid.

Touched by Holy Heartache

In the garden where sorrow's grown,
We find the seeds of love we've sown.
Touched by heartache, grace takes flight,
In darkest valleys, we seek the light.

Through aching winds, a voice reveals,
In every wound, a truth it seals.
With open palms, we carry pain,
Yet in the hurt, love shall remain.

The holy tear, a sacred stream,
From loss emerges the purest dream.
In broken paths, we walk as one,
For in the night, it's love that shone.

Each heartache bears a holy weight,
In the stillness, our souls await.
For through our trials, the spirit grows,
In every ache, the heart bestows.

So let us stand, though storms may roar,
For in the hurt, we seek even more.
Touched by heartache, we'll rise and sing,
In every loss, new life will spring.

Yearning Among the Saints

In hallowed halls where shadows lie,
The whispers of the righteous sigh.
Their prayers ascend like fragrant smoke,
A bond unbroken, a promise spoke.

Hearts entwined in sacred grace,
In each dawn, we seek His face.
With every tear, a hope reborn,
In holy love, we are not torn.

The angels gather, wings unfurled,
To comfort souls in a weary world.
Through trials set, our faith remains,
In silent prayers, we bear our chains.

United still in love divine,
We seek His strength, and in Him, shine.
As saints above look down with care,
Their guiding light, our constant prayer.

Together we strive, hand in hand,
In grace we walk, across the land.
In every heart, His love will soar,
Yearning among the saints, forevermore.

Twilight of the Last Embrace

Beneath the stars, where dreams reside,
In twilight's glow, we search inside.
The veil between the worlds grows thin,
In silent thoughts, our souls begin.

With every heartbeat close we stand,
In shadows cast by His loving hand.
A final breath, a whispered prayer,
In the last embrace, He'll always care.

The nightingale sings a sorrowed tune,
As hope ascends beneath the moon.
In every ending, light will start,
For love transcends, uniting hearts.

The whispers echo, eternal bliss,
In sacred moments, we find His kiss.
Each tear we shed, a testament true,
In twilight's grace, we're born anew.

When dawn breaks forth, we'll rise again,
Embracing light, our only gain.
For in His love, we find our place,
In the twilight of the last embrace.

The Last Supper of Forgotten Affection

At the table set with quiet grace,
We gather 'round, each sacred face.
In bread and wine, the past returns,
With every heart, a memory burns.

The laughter shared, a love once bright,
Now echoes faint in the dimming light.
Yet still we hold, though time may stray,
In gentle whispers, we find our way.

With each embrace, a hint of sorrow,
Yet hope abides for a new tomorrow.
In every bite, the taste of grace,
In the silent love, we find our place.

Though paths may part, the bonds remain,
In reverence spoken, joy and pain.
For in this meal, our souls connect,
In the last supper, we still reflect.

And when we rise after the feast,
We carry forth, peace to the least.
In forgotten affection, life's sweet refrain,
Will guide us home through joy and pain.

A Refuge for the Broken Spirit

In valleys low, where shadows creep,
A refuge waits, a promise deep.
He gathers close the weary soul,
In gentle hands, we find our whole.

With every burden, He bears the weight,
Restoring hopes, He heals our fate.
Through storms that rage and tempests call,
In His embrace, we rise from all.

The wounded heart knows love's sweet balm,
In sacred peace, we find our calm.
Each whispered prayer, a soft embrace,
Within His arms, we find our place.

When darkness falls, our light remains,
In quiet strength, He breaks our chains.
No longer lost, we stand renewed,
In refuge found, our path is true.

So to the broken, near or far,
Remember well, just who you are.
For in His name, we find our way,
A refuge for the broken, come what may.

The Way of the Faithful Yet Faded

In shadows cast by ancient time,
A whisper calls, a distant chime.
Forsaken paths where once we trod,
Now silent, lost, the voice of God.

The trembling hearts in twilight's glow,
Seek solace where the rivers flow.
Yet pain and doubt weave through their prayer,
As fleeting souls drift on despair.

In sorrow's dance, they find their song,
For even broken, they belong.
With faith that flickers, dimly bright,
They yearn for truth, for guiding light.

The weary gaze upon the dawn,
With hopes that rise when night is gone.
Through burdens borne in love's embrace,
They walk the way of faded grace.

Yet in their hearts, a spark remains,
The echo of eternal flames.
In every tear, in every sigh,
A testament to faith that'll not die.

Soliloquy of Sorrowful Grace

In gardens where the lilies weep,
A heart in anguish learns to seep.
The petals fall like whispered dreams,
In twilight's hush, the silence screams.

Oh gentle breeze, why dost thou sigh,
With memories of days gone by?
The grace of love, once vibrant, bold,
Now wraps the soul in shrouds of cold.

Beneath the arch of heaven's dome,
There dwells a heart that finds no home.
With every prayer that bids goodbye,
A mournful hymn that drifts and sighs.

Yet through the shadows, light does break,
A flicker for the lost heart's sake.
In vulnerability, they soar,
Finding strength in love's true core.

With pen in hand, the tale unfolds,
Of sorrow turned to grace that holds.
Through grief and pain, the spirit finds,
A love eternal that never blinds.

The Consequence of Celestial Desires

Beneath the stars, dreams intertwine,
An echo of a love divine.
Yet in their grasp, the heavens strain,
For longing hearts invite their pain.

To reach for skies both bright and vast,
The heart must bear its heavy past.
In search of truth, they wade through night,
Chasing visions, fading light.

Each wish a thread in fate's design,
Yet tangled hopes leave scars that shine.
In celestial paths, the soul must tread,
A cost of longing, tears unsaid.

When dreams collide with harshest fate,
And whispers turn to cries of hate.
The consequence that hearts must face,
Is love, though fleeting, a warm embrace.

Yet still they yearn for stars to guide,
In every tempest, they confide.
Through cosmic dance, they seek to find,
A sacred peace in hearts entwined.

Hymn of the Damned Heart

Oh burdened soul, in shadows cast,
What echoes haunt you from the past?
In chains of regret, your spirit cries,
A doomed hymn sung 'neath empty skies.

With every tear, a verse is penned,
A ballad lost that has no end.
Yet in the depth, a flicker glows,
A strength within that seldom shows.

The silence shrouds your mournful plea,
Yet hope awaits on bended knee.
In every heart that feels the ache,
A melody that dawn can't break.

Though darkness wields its cruelest grasp,
In every pain, a hand to clasp.
The hymn of those who dwell in night,
Resounds with dreams of dawn's bright light.

So sing, dear heart, despite the scars,
For in the void, there lie the stars.
A testament to battles fought,
A divine path that sorrow wrought.

Thorns of an Unholy Affection

In shadows where the longing dwells,
The heart is bound, a soul in hell.
With whispers sweet, yet poison near,
Thorns of love, we learn to fear.

A gaze that burns, a touch that stains,
In sacred halls, where love remains.
Yet darkness wraps the heart's embrace,
An unholy path we dare to trace.

The altar set with prayers unheard,
In silence, hearts are gently stirred.
The thorns grow deep, they pierce the skin,
A love that's lost, where sin begins.

Yet still we chase the fleeting grace,
Through twisted paths, we seek a place.
With faith as light, we walk this road,
In thorns of love, our hearts bestowed.

And when we fall, the angels weep,
For unholy promises we keep.
In every sigh, a prayer does rise,
As we confront our own demise.

The Lament of the Unrequited

In twilight's hush, my heart does ache,
For love unreturned, a bitter stake.
I seek the gaze that shies away,
A fleeting glance, but gone astray.

With every prayer, a tear I shed,
In dreams of you, my spirit's bled.
The sacred voice that calls my name,
Yet leaves my soul in endless shame.

A yearning deep, like rivers flow,
In silence kept, my sorrows grow.
With whispered hopes, I tread the night,
For love unclaimed, a fading light.

I walk in shadows, shunned and lost,
In faith I pay the heavy cost.
But still I toil, for hearts must mend,
In solemn prayers, my soul to send.

Yet in this void, there lies a spark,
A flicker found within the dark.
Though unrequited, I shall stand,
For love remains, by God's own hand.

Blessings Woven with Grief

In tapestry of joy and pain,
Life's blessings come, like gentle rain.
With every thread, both bright and dark,
We weave a tale, an endless arc.

Each tear we drop, a sacred gift,
In sorrow's arms, our spirits lift.
The burdens shared in whispered grace,
Bring forth the light in our embrace.

For in the grief, the blessings hide,
A sacred truth, we cannot bide.
In silence grand, we find the song,
That guides us through where hearts belong.

With every heartbeat, love is spun,
In trials faced, we come undone.
Yet woven tight, our dreams entwined,
In blessing's name, our hearts aligned.

So let us dance within the strife,
For blessings bloom where there is life.
In sorrow's wake, let joy be found,
In sacred knots, our souls unbound.

Shattered Vows and Holy Writ

In sacred books, the words are clear,
Yet shattered vows bring forth the fear.
The promises made beneath the skies,
In whispered dreams, now slowly die.

With trembling hands, we write our fate,
The holy path, we hesitate.
In shadows deep, where trust is lost,
We count the price, we bear the cost.

In every heart, the echoes call,
Of love once strong, now bound to fall.
Yet still we seek the light to mend,
Through ashes left, on hope depend.

For every vow that breaks apart,
A lesson learned, a brand new start.
In faith we rise, though hearts may quake,
For in the grief, new chains we break.

So let us hold the holy writ,
In shattered dreams, our souls commit.
To rise again, from dust we bloom,
In love's great name, dispelling gloom.

The Gospel of Longing

In the stillness of my heart, I pray,
Longing whispers, guiding my way.
Hope shines brightly through the night,
Leading my soul towards the light.

Tears like rain fall gently down,
Washing me free from this crown.
With every wish, I seek Your grace,
Yearning to find a sacred space.

In the echoes of a quiet plea,
I search for truth, a glimpse of Thee.
Each moment holds a promise dear,
To fill the void I hold so near.

Within the shadows, I await,
For love divine to guide my fate.
With hands outstretched and heart aglow,
I walk the path where longings flow.

Embrace my struggles, cleanse my fear,
In every sigh, Lord, You are near.
This gospel of longing speaks aloud,
In faith, I stand, forever bowed.

A Confession to the Heavens

With trembling hands, I lift my voice,
In quiet moments, I make my choice.
To bare my soul, I seek the light,
Confessing sins that haunt the night.

Oh, heavens wide, hear my lament,
Each burdened thought, a heart that's spent.
Forgive the shadows that I've known,
Transform my pain to seeds that've grown.

In every tear, a story lies,
Fragments of faith, where hope defies.
Lift me up from this weary plight,
Help me find strength in Your true light.

As whispers rise, like incense sweet,
I stand before Thee at Your feet.
My sins laid bare, my heart so pure,
In Your embrace, Lord, I'll endure.

I seek redemption, hear my call,
A confession made, I give my all.
In heavenly grace, I find my peace,
With each new dawn, my worries cease.

The Covenant of Silent Suffering

In silence deep, where shadows dwell,
A covenant forged, a sacred shell.
Suffering whispers secrets low,
In trials faced, Your love will grow.

Each pain a thread in beauty's loom,
Weaving strength from heart's great tomb.
In solitude, my spirit learns,
From darkness, light forever burns.

Oh, suffering, You speak so clear,
In every ache, a truth appears.
Through trials past and burdens borne,
The heart rejoices in the morn.

This silent pact, I now embrace,
For in my wounds, I find Your grace.
A covenant made through tears and strife,
In every struggle, I see life.

Come, Lord, and guide my weary soul,
Through silent suffering, make me whole.
In every tear, a chance to grow,
I walk in faith, where love will flow.

Hymns of Distant Affection

Across the skies, my heart does soar,
In distant lands, I search for more.
With hymns of love, I call Your name,
In every note, the flame remains.

Oh, distant stars, bear witness true,
My affection flows, a deep adieu.
Though miles apart, our souls entwine,
In sacred rhythms, love divine.

Through trials faced, my heart does ache,
Each melody, a path I take.
With every song, a prayer takes flight,
Guiding my spirit through the night.

In every echo, whispers blend,
A bond unbroken, without end.
Though far away, You feel so near,
In hymns of distant love, I cheer.

A melody of hope I sing,
For love, dear Lord, is everything.
In every heartbeat, in each refrain,
Distant affection, the eternal gain.

Grappling with Divine Arguments

Beneath the heavens, I seek to understand,
Questions arise as I reach for Your hand.
Silent whispers echo through night,
Divine secrets hidden from my sight.

In prayerful turmoil, my spirit bends,
Each answered call brings more amends.
Must I wrestle in shadows to find grace,
Or is it in struggle that I see Your face?

The stars align, yet doubts linger still,
As I ascend the mountain, I climb with will.
Your presence, a beacon through the haze,
Guiding the heart through tumultuous days.

In gardens of faith, I toil and sow,
Seeking the truth in each seed I throw.
And though the weeds of skepticism sprout,
I stand firm, my faith will carry me out.

So let my heart cry out in the night,
For in the darkest moments, I see Your light.
With each divine argument that I face,
I find Your promise, my sacred place.

The Scripture of Lost Promises

In ancient texts, I trace the lines,
Profound stories of love that binds.
Yet in the margins, hope has bled,
With ink of sorrow, on pages read.

Whispers of promises softly break,
In shadows cast by choices I make.
Every verse a heartbeat, every sigh,
In search of a truth that will never die.

The ink may fade, but the spirit remains,
Binding my heart through losses and gains.
Every struggle, each tear I shed,
A reminder of the words left unsaid.

In the silence, I feel the weight,
Of lost agreements, a heavy fate.
Yet even in sorrow, a thread does weave,
A tapestry of hope, that we can believe.

As I ponder, the pages turn,
With every loss, a lesson to learn.
The scripture of promises lost in time,
Reveals the journey, a sacred rhyme.

Prayers Caught in the Winds of Change

In the stillness, I raise my voice,
To the heavens, I make my choice.
Each prayer a feather, caught in flight,
Whirling away into the night.

The winds of change, they shift and sway,
Carrying hopes that stray away.
Yet in the tempest, I find my ground,
In every gust, Your grace is found.

I cast my cares upon the breeze,
Trusting in You, my soul finds ease.
Through darkened skies, I learn to trust,
That in Your hands, I am but dust.

With every shadow, a flicker of light,
Leading me onward, through fears of the night.
For in the change, Your love is clear,
A steady whisper to calm my fear.

So I sail these winds, both wild and free,
With prayers that echo, "Bind me to Thee."
Through every season, my spirit sings,
Embraced by the joy that change truly brings.

Tenebrous Affection

In shadows deep, affection hides,
A tender love that still abides.
Through veils of darkness, whispers roam,
Seeking solace in a weary home.

Hands outstretched in muted grace,
Finding warmth in a cold embrace.
In every silence, my heart calls out,
A tenebrous affection, wrapped in doubt.

The stars above veil their light,
Yet even in darkness, love ignites.
Though fears may grip with icy hands,
Hope blooms gently in sacred lands.

With shadows dancing, I dare to dream,
In twilight's glow, love becomes a theme.
A tapestry woven of joy and pain,
Through tenebrous nights, there's much to gain.

So let the night blanket my soul,
In love's embrace, I find my whole.
For in the darkness, affection so real,
Transforms the shadows, breathing zeal.

Pilgrimage Through Tender Regrets

On winding roads my heart does roam,
Seeking solace, far from home.
Each step a whisper of the past,
In shadows cast, my sorrows last.

With every tear that clouds the dawn,
The memories dance, yet I move on.
In gardens where the lilies weep,
I find the lessons life doth keep.

The stars above, a guiding light,
Illuminate the paths of night.
Each regret, a silent prayer,
Laid softly at the altar there.

Through valleys low, I lift my gaze,
Embracing hope, refusing haze.
The journey long, yet here I stand,
Held gently by a loving hand.

So gently treads this fragile heart,
In faith and love, we barely part.
In every whisper, tender grace,
I find my strength, my resting place.

Lamentations of the Forsaken

In shadows deep where silence reigns,
The echoes of forgotten names.
With heavy hearts, we mourn the lost,
Bearing the wounds of love's great cost.

The winds do carry a mournful tune,
Under the watch of a pale moon.
Every sigh a prayer in flight,
Yearning for comfort through the night.

Forsaken souls with silent cries,
Longing for hope beyond the skies.
In hidden corners, burdens lie,
As spirits broken, we comply.

Yet in our grief, we find a spark,
A flicker bright within the dark.
From ashes rise, a tale to weave,
In sorrow's depth, we shall believe.

So let us sing through tear-filled eyes,
A song of strength that never dies.
For in lament, we find our song,
A chorus bold, a heart made strong.

Intercessions for a Distant Heart

Beneath the stars, I seek your peace,
A prayer for love that will not cease.
Across the miles, the longing grows,
In quiet moments, the spirit knows.

Each whisper calls, a fervent plea,
To bridge the gap, just you and me.
With every breath, my heart does yearn,
For chance to feel the love we've earned.

In solitude, the tears have flowed,
A path of faith we have both strode.
Yet love remains a guiding star,
Though skies may darken, you're never far.

So I arise, my spirit light,
With intercessions through the night.
For distant hearts can still unite,
On wings of hope, we soar in flight.

Let souls entwine with sacred grace,
In every tear, your sweet embrace.
For love, though far, shall never wane,
Together still, we break the chain.

The Divine Embrace of Pain

In every wound, a lesson found,
Where pain does guide, and hopes abound.
The struggle fierce, yet shadows pass,
Through fiery trials, we shall amass.

With every tear, pure strength emerges,
In darkened seas, my spirit surges.
Though pierced by thorns, I see the bloom,
In suffering sown, I feel the room.

The heart does ache, yet finds its song,
In silent echoes, where we belong.
For in my anguish, I can see,
The path to grace is set for me.

So let the storms of life arise,
For in my struggle, I grow wise.
Each scar a mark of love's design,
In every ache, a glimpse divine.

Thus, through the fire, I walk unshaken,
In pain's embrace, my spirit awaken.
With every breath, I rise anew,
In love's embrace, I am made true.

Broken Halos and Wishful Thinking

In the silence where whispers dwell,
Hope flickers in the hollow shell.
Angels cry for dreams once bright,
Now shadowed beneath the night.

Lost in prayers, we search for light,
A broken halo, a fading sight.
Yet the heart beats with desire,
For wishful thinking to inspire.

We gather stones of shattered grace,
In broken paths, we seek our place.
Hands raised high, we plead and yearn,
For the lessons life must turn.

Among the thorns, a flower grows,
From troubled soil, compassion flows.
In every scar, a testimony,
We find strength in the agony.

As dawn unfolds, the shadows flee,
In broken wings, we find the key.
With every tear, a seed is sown,
From wishful thoughts, new hope is grown.

The Sermon of Lost Embrace

In the stillness of the evening light,
We gather here to seek the right.
Voices linger in the air,
Echoes of love and silent prayer.

With open hearts, we share our pain,
Every loss, a sacred gain.
Embraces lost, yet never gone,
In memories, we carry on.

The burdens felt, yet not displayed,
In shadows, a light is laid.
Through the fog of despair's embrace,
We find solace, a holy space.

The call of faith, though faint at times,
Reminds us through the darkest climes.
For every tear that's ever shed,
A gift of grace, the spirit fed.

Let us rise from depths of ache,
With fervent prayers the heavens shake.
In the bonds of love, we find our way,
In every heart, a bright array.

Though lost embraces mark our days,
The spirit's warmth forever stays.
In unity, we find our peace,
In the sermon of love, our fears release.

Shadows on the Sacred Ground

In fields where faith was surely sown,
We walk the paths, yet feel alone.
Shadows dance upon the earth,
Whispering tales of love and worth.

Beneath the veil of twilight's grace,
We search for hope in this holy space.
Footsteps echo, faint yet bold,
In sacred stories yet untold.

The spirit's breath upon our face,
A gentle touch, a warm embrace.
When shadows linger, faith will rise,
In every heart, the truth lies.

Yet trials come like storms at sea,
Testing the soul, setting it free.
Through darkest nights, we find the light,
In shadows cast, our spirits fight.

With every prayer, we plant a seed,
In sacred ground, our souls are freed.
Together we find the strength to stand,
With shadows mingling, hand in hand.

Benedictions of the Wounded

In every wound, a story breathes,
In every ache, a heart believes.
Through trials faced and battles fought,
In prayers, solace is sought.

Benedictions fall like gentle rain,
Healing waters wash away pain.
Let the spirit mend what's torn,
From brokenness, we are reborn.

In the silence, where sorrows dwell,
We learn to rise, we learn to tell.
Each scar, a mark of what we've braved,
In every soul, a promise saved.

Compassion flows like a river wide,
In every heart where love can bide.
The wounded share their tender grace,
In unity, we find our place.

With open hands, we lift each voice,
In the face of pain, we make our choice.
Let every tear be a sacred prayer,
In benedictions, we find care.

Together we walk this sacred path,
In every struggle, in every wrath.
For in our wounds, we find the truth,
Benedictions of the wounded youth.

Gospel of the Forgotten

In whispers low, the lost ones call,
Their shadows dance, where echoes fall.
From ancient texts, the truth unfolds,
In search of light, their story told.

In every heart, a prayer resides,
A seed of hope that never hides.
Through trials faced, they find their way,
In silent nights, they seek the day.

Forgiveness shines like morning dew,
Transforming pain to love anew.
The forgotten ones, they rise and sing,
In unity, their voices ring.

With faith as strong as mountain stone,
They gather close, no longer alone.
Through tears and laughter, life prevails,
Their gospel spreads like ancient trails.

In grace they walk, the burden light,
For every soul can find the right.
The forgotten, now a guiding star,
In the heavens, they shine from afar.

Lessons from an Imperfect God

In shadows deep, the stories spin,
Of a Creator shaped by sin.
With tender hands, He molds our clay,
And finds His joy in flaws displayed.

With every crack, a lesson told,
In brokenness, His love unfolds.
For in our hearts, frail hopes abide,
Imperfect grace, our constant guide.

Through shattered dreams, the light breaks through,
A gentle touch, a chance to renew.
In every stumble, wisdom shared,
The lessons learned, the love declared.

He walks with us in darkest nights,
Embracing pain with endless light.
For even gods can bear regrets,
In loving hands, our fate connects.

With open hearts, we find our way,
No perfect path, yet bright the day.
Through all the flaws, we rise and stand,
In every heart, He holds our hand.

The Soul's Sanctuary of Regret

In silent corners, shadows blend,
Where whispered truths and sorrows mend.
Each choice we make, a step away,
In sanctuary, regret holds sway.

With heavy hearts, we weave our tales,
Of dreams that missed, of breathless gales.
But in the pain, a lesson lies,
For in the dark, our spirit tries.

Through fragile hopes, we bear the weight,
The soul's abode, a realm of fate.
In every tear, a tale unfolds,
As love and loss, the heart upholds.

In quiet moments, stillness reigns,
The tapestry of joy and pains.
Regret, a guide on paths we roam,
A sacred space that leads us home.

Embrace the ache, the softest burn,
For every wound, a chance to learn.
In sanctuary, we find our peace,
And through the storm, our hearts release.

Meditations in a Garden of Sorrows

In gardens lush, where shadows play,
The weight of sorrow finds its way.
Petals fall like dreams unmade,
In whispered winds, our hearts are swayed.

We walk through paths of silver dew,
With every step, the pain feels new.
Yet in each thorn, a beauty grows,
In silent grace, the spirit knows.

Beneath the boughs, the stillness reigns,
In every heart, the echo remains.
Through seasons turning, we reflect,
In gardens deep, our souls connect.

With open arms, we greet the night,
The moon her watchful gaze ignites.
In meditation, sorrows bloom,
A testament to love's perfume.

In this embrace of dusk and dawn,
We find the strength to carry on.
For in the garden, pain is sown,
In every heart, compassion grown.

The Sorrowful Mysteries of Affection

In shadows cast by silent night,
The heart weeps soft, a gentle plight.
Each tear's a prayer unto the sky,
For love, though lost, will never die.

Upon the altar of despair,
Resilience blooms in whispered prayer.
Through every trial, faith will rise,
In sorrow's depth, true love defies.

Beneath the burden of the cross,
We find the beauty in the loss.
A journey paved with thorns and grace,
In each embrace, we find His face.

Thus, let the broken hearts unite,
In the stillness of the night.
For even in the depths of pain,
A sacred love will still remain.

So lift your eyes, though heavy the load,
In every trial, we walk this road.
Embrace the mysteries, grim yet bright,
For sorrow leads us to the light.

Echoes of Celestial Grief

When angels weep and shadows fade,
The heart's lament in silence laid.
Each echo speaks of love's pure might,
In the darkened depth, they shed their light.

The stars align in sorrow's dance,
With every sigh, a fleeting chance.
Across the heavens, tears descend,
A testament that time won't end.

For every loss, a memory shared,
In longing hearts, our anguish bared.
Yet in this sorrow, hope persists,
In every prayer, our spirits twist.

Lost in the whispers of the night,
We search for solace in the flight.
The celestial hues of grief can fade,
Yet love remains, unafraid, displayed.

In the quiet, where echoes dwell,
We find the strength in sorrow's spell.
For through the grief, a love will soar,
In heaven's arms, forevermore.

Whispers of the Fallen Heart

In twilight's hush, a heart does break,
Soft whispers rise, the soul awake.
In every passing breath, we mourn,
The love once cherished now is torn.

Yet in this sorrow, grace does gleam,
A faint whisper of a dream.
Through every tear, a story's told,
In love's embrace, we find the bold.

The fallen heart finds strength anew,
In gentle winds, a love so true.
For in the fragments, light does shine,
A sacred bond, forever divine.

Though shadows linger, hope remains,
In deepest pain, true love still gains.
As stars above begin to weep,
We gather love in faith to keep.

So let the whispers fill the air,
In every moment, feel the care.
For though the heart may fall and ache,
A resurrected love we'll make.

Temptations of the Sacred Tear

When tempests rage and hearts are sore,
The sacred tear, it seeks the shore.
A testament of trials faced,
In every drop, the grace is traced.

In moments dark, we find the light,
As prayers ascend into the night.
The sacred tear, pure as the dove,
Reflects the depth of boundless love.

Yet temptations whisper, try to bind,
In every sorrow, seek and find.
For though we fall, we rise again,
In each embrace, our faith shall reign.

Through valleys deep, the spirits soar,
In pain and joy, we are restored.
A tear may fall, but hope shall gleam,
In every challenge, we will dream.

So let the sacred tears be known,
In every heart, the seeds are sown.
With every storm, we walk in grace,
In love's embrace, we find our place.

A Psalm for the Brokenhearted

In silence, my heart cries out to You,
For in this storm, my spirit's torn anew.
Yet in the darkness, Your light shall reign,
With every tear, You embrace my pain.

Through valleys deep, I wander alone,
Each step a prayer, my heart now a stone.
But Your gentle whisper calls me near,
Restoring hope, calming every fear.

The weight of sorrow, a heavy chain,
Yet in my weakness, Your strength remains.
You lift my soul from despair's cold grasp,
In Your sweet mercy, my heart finds rest.

In the midst of ashes, beauty grows,
From broken dreams, a river flows.
You mend my heart and set it free,
In every heartache, a love for Thee.

I rise again, a phoenix in flight,
With faith as my cloak, I'll seek Your light.
For in this journey, I find my song,
A Psalm for the broken calls me along.

Light Through Cracked Vessels

In every vessel cracked and worn,
Your light seeps through, a hope reborn.
Though fragments fall on the path I tread,
You fill the spaces, where darkness led.

A potter's hand shapes each fragile soul,
With every fracture, You make me whole.
In humble offerings, my spirit glows,
Through brokenness, true beauty shows.

As dawn breaks softly on weary skies,
Your grace descends in sweet replies.
With tender hands, You mend my seams,
Transforming my heart, igniting dreams.

Let not my ashes define my fate,
For through the cracks, I lift my plate.
In gratitude, my praises soar,
You are the light I can't ignore.

With every heartbeat, Your love will guide,
In cracked vessels, You will abide.
Even in shadows, I see the bright,
Forever I'll follow, Your purest light.

The Path of Thorned Roses

Upon this path where roses grow,
Thorns pierce soft flesh, and beauty glows.
Yet with each step, I learn to dance,
In trials faced, there's not just chance.

The fragrance sweet, a gift from pain,
Life blooms in storms; joy comes with rain.
For every thorn, a lesson learned,
In fiery trials, my heart has yearned.

Through valleys dark, with courage bold,
In every struggle, a story told.
The path I've walked, though steep with strife,
Is woven close with threads of life.

Yet still I rise beneath the sun,
In thorned embrace, my hope's begun.
For every hardship bears a flower,
A testament to Love's great power.

With gratitude, I face my way,
In thorned roses, I shall not sway.
For on this journey, I am shown,
That through the pain, I have grown.

Sanctity in Solitude

In quiet moments, I seek Your face,
In solitude, I find Your grace.
With every heartbeat, whispers arise,
In sacred stillness, my spirit flies.

Away from noise, the world retreats,
In silent praise, my essence meets.
Each breath a hymn, each thought a prayer,
In solitude's arms, I find You there.

The quiet depths, a well of peace,
In every stillness, my fears release.
Here in the shadows, I see the light,
Your love surrounds me, pure and bright.

With open heart, I yield to Thee,
In solitude's embrace, I'm truly free.
Each moment cherished, a sacred bond,
In the depths of silence, I respond.

So lead me deeper, away from strife,
In sanctity, I find true life.
For in the quiet, I hear the call,
To be renewed and to stand tall.

Psalm of a Sorrowful Soul

In shadows deep where silence dwells,
A broken heart with secrets tells,
Oh Lord, hear my lamenting cry,
For in this pain, my spirit sighs.

The tears I shed, like rivers flow,
To cleanse the wounds, my soul's deep woe,
Upon the altar of despair,
I lay my burdens, frail and bare.

In darkest nights, Your light may fade,
Yet still, I seek the hope You made,
With every breath, I call Your name,
Rescue me from this silent shame.

Each whispered prayer, a fragile thread,
In weary arms of love, I'm led,
Though valleys low my spirit knows,
Your grace sustains, the heart still grows.

So lift me high where eagles soar,
And in Your strength, I'll fear no more,
My sorrowed soul, to You I yield,
In faith's embrace, my heart is healed.

Rituals of Wounded Trust

In sacred space, we gather near,
With hearts laid bare, we shed our fear,
A fragile bond, once forged in light,
Now bends beneath the weight of night.

I offer prayers, on petals strewn,
For memories that fade too soon,
An oath once spoken, now forlorn,
In shadows cast, our trust is torn.

We lift our voices, a mournful song,
Together trembling, righting wrongs,
With open hands, we face the truth,
In broken vows, we reclaim youth.

Each ritual bound, our spirits chase,
The whispers lost, in sacred grace,
Let mercy rain, the heart restore,
In unity, we heal once more.

So cleanse us, Lord, with tides of love,
As spirits rise, on wings above,
Through wounds of trust, we find our way,
In faith renewed, we learn to pray.

Resurrecting the Fallen Heart

In ashes cold, where dreams once lay,
I search for light to guide my way,
Oh Lord, revive this weary soul,
From shattered thoughts, make the whole.

The echoes of a life before,
Resound like thunder on the shore,
Yet in the silence, I will wait,
For You, oh God, control my fate.

With gentle hands, You mold the clay,
In every trial, I bend and sway,
From brokenness, new life shall grow,
An altar built on love I know.

As petals bloom from winter's chill,
I trust in You, my heart will fill,
From darkness drawn, into the light,
You lift me high, my spirit bright.

Resurrected now, I stand in grace,
With every heartbeat, I embrace,
The joy that comes with faith restored,
In You, my Savior, I'm adored.

The Soliloquy of a Desperate Prayer

In quiet moments, I confide,
My restless heart, it cannot hide,
Oh Lord, I seek Your calming hand,
In silence here, I make my stand.

With every breath, I call to You,
In sacred whispers, hopes renew,
Each tear a message, sent above,
A language known, of deepest love.

Through valleys dark, my spirit weeps,
Yet in Your promise, solace keeps,
A prayer once small, now towers high,
In faith's embrace, I learn to fly.

The shadows dance, the doubts may grow,
But through the storm, Your light will show,
In desperate cries, I find my song,
For in Your joy, I do belong.

So hear my plea, Oh gentle Lord,
In every breath, let hope be poured,
And as I kneel, my heart laid bare,
I find my peace in desperate prayer.

Beneath the Veil of Silent Suffering

In shadows deep, where silence weeps,
The heartache gathers, the spirit keeps.
With weary hands and prayerful sighs,
Beneath the veil, the sorrow lies.

A whisper stirs, a hope divine,
Through darkest nights, the stars align.
Each tear that falls, a sacred rite,
In pain, we find the path to light.

For every wound, a lesson learned,
From ashes, faith's bright ember burned.
The soul, though bruised, shall rise again,
So rise, dear heart, from silent pain.

With every breath, a prayer ascends,
United spirits, the broken mend.
In burdens shared, the love entwines,
Through suffering, the heart defines.

Beneath the veil, we shall not stay,
For in our trials, we find the way.
The light within will break the night,
In silent suffering, we find our might.

Anointed with Regret

A crown of thorns, a heart of stone,
In sacred wells, our sins are sown.
Each shadow cast, a tale untold,
Anointed with regret, yet bold.

The whispers haunt, a lingering breath,
In quiet moments, we dance with death.
The choice of love or bitter divide,
In every tear, the truth must hide.

Regrets, like chains, we wear them tight,
Yet through remorse, we seek the light.
The path of sorrow leads to grace,
In every fall, a warm embrace.

A broken heart shall find its song,
Through every note, we all belong.
In every scar, a story lies,
Anointed, we rise, beneath the skies.

To scatter seeds of hope and love,
In hand with faith, we rise above.
For in our flaws, perfection gleams,
Through anointed paths, we chase our dreams.

The Ashes of a Forgotten Embrace

In twilight's grip, we softly tread,
On whispers lost, this love long dead.
The ashes soft, like dreams that fade,
In forgotten embrace, our hearts betrayed.

Each memory drifts, like smoke in air,
With heavy hearts, we learn to care.
The echoes speak of times once shared,
In silence deep, the soul is bared.

Yet from the dust, a phoenix flies,
Through sorrow's depth, our spirit sighs.
In every loss, a chance to grow,
From ashes stirred, new fires glow.

A candle's flame shall light the night,
In darkened halls, we chase the light.
Though love may fade, we stand our ground,
In every heartbeat, hope is found.

The past may linger, but we will rise,
With wings of faith, we touch the skies.
The ashes tell of battles won,
In love's embrace, we are reborn.

Celestial Tears in an Earthly Realm

In heavens high, the stars bleed blue,
Celestial tears that fall like dew.
They grace the earth, a sacred gift,
In sorrow's path, our souls they lift.

Each droplet speaks of pain long borne,
A cosmic dance, where dreams are torn.
Yet in the depths, a light breaks through,
In every tear, the hope shines true.

The realms of grief, we wander far,
While angels weep beneath the stars.
Their songs resonate, a healing balm,
In earthly strife, we find the calm.

Through trials faced, we learn to see,
The beauty held in tragedy.
For in each tear, a prayer ascends,
In cosmic love, our heart defends.

So let the tears nourish the ground,
In earthly realm, the joy is found.
Celestial bonds, forever strong,
Through every sorrow, we belong.

Echoes of an Atoning Heart

In the silence of the night, we plead,
Whispers of sorrow, the soul's true need.
Each tear a prayer, each heartbeat a song,
Echoes of love where we once belonged.

From depths of despair, we search for grace,
A path of redemption, we long to embrace.
Forgiveness blooms in the gardens of time,
In the light of the dawn, our spirits will climb.

Oh, sacred vessel, hold our regrets,
In your warm cradle, our burden resets.
Let healing waters flow softly and pure,
In the arms of the mercy, our hearts will endure.

We dance with shadows, embrace the past,
In memories' arms, our shadows are cast.
Each echo a promise, each sigh a wish,
In the light of atonement, we find our bliss.

Together we stand, united in pain,
With whispers of hope, we rise once again.
An atoning heart, in its purest form,
Whispers of faith through the darkest storm.

Sacrifices at the Altar of Desire

At the altar of longing, we kneel and cry,
With offerings of dreams, we reach for the sky.
Each wish a candle, each hope a refrain,
Sacrifices made in love's gentle name.

Beneath the weight of desire's own flame,
Our hearts weave together, yet feel the same.
What we seek often slips through our hands,
Yet faith holds us tight in life's shifting sands.

As the sun sets low on the horizon's edge,
We promise our souls on life's sacred pledge.
Each whisper of want, a prayer softly said,
On the altar of desire, love's hunger bred.

In shadows of yearning, our spirits entwine,
With sacrifices made, our hearts are divine.
Through trials of longing, we learn to be whole,
In the dance of passion, we find our true role.

Let the aroma of hope fill the night air,
As stars become watchers, hear our humble prayer.
In the glow of devotion, we rise from the floor,
Sacrifices honored, our spirits will soar.

The Prayer of Empty Arms

In the stillness of night, a prayer takes flight,
For empty arms longing with all of their might.
A silence echoes where love should reside,
With each whispered hope, we reach for the tide.

Under moonlight's gaze, we search for a sign,
An answer to questions, a heart that aligns.
With palms turned to heaven, we yearn to embrace,
The warmth of affection, the soft touch of grace.

Yet void still remains in this silent hour,
A longing unfurling like a delicate flower.
Each heartbeat a memory, each sigh a soft plea,
In the hush of the night, it's Your love we seek.

Through trials of distance, we learn to let go,
In the vastness of longing, our spirits will grow.
So lift up these voices, let them pierce the dark,
With faith in our hearts, we carry the spark.

In time's gentle arms, our wishes will find,
The treasures of love that were left behind.
For empty arms cradle a hope yet untold,
This prayer for connection, forever bold.

Divine Shadows of Lost Affection

In the garden of memory, shadows grow deep,
Divine revelations that silence our sleep.
Each petal that falls bears witness to pain,
In the echoes of laughter, love's tender refrain.

Lost affection lingers in whispers of grace,
A waltz of remembrance that time can't erase.
With every heartbeat, our stories unfold,
In the light of the spirit, we find what we hold.

Yet beneath the surface, a river flows wide,
Of all that we cherished, of love we can't hide.
In the shadowed corners, we learn to forgive,
Through the dance of acceptance, we learn how to live.

As dusk settles low, we gather the nights,
To weave together our fragmented sights.
In the tapestry of time, the threads intertwine,
Each shadow a story, beautifully divine.

So let us remember the love that we shared,
In divine shadows, no heart is ensnared.
Though affection may fade, its essence remains,
In the hearts of the faithful, love's light ever reigns.

Rapture Lost in Time

In shadows deep, we search for grace,
Eluding hands that grasp at space.
Whispers of hope, in silence roam,
Yet distant dreams will lead us home.

The clock ticks on, with fervent breath,
Each fleeting moment hints of death.
Yet in the void, a light does gleam,
Awakening hearts to the unseen dream.

A tapestry of trials spun,
Threads of anguish, woven in one.
Yet faith ignites a glowing spark,
Illuminating paths from dark.

In timeless echoes, spirits sigh,
Rapture escapes, yet we must try.
To seize the dawn, though lost in night,
Embracing love, our guiding light.

With every tear, a lesson wakes,
Through cosmic storms, the soul partakes.
In every loss, a chance to see,
The rapture that sets our spirits free.

The Covenant of Withered Roses

Amidst the thorns, a promise lies,
In petals soft, where beauty dies.
A solemn vow, to honor pain,
In fragrant air, love blooms again.

Withered yet wise, the roses stand,
Holding secrets in nature's hand.
A covenant forged in silent tears,
Transcending all of our fleeting years.

Each fragrance whispers of the past,
Of joys that lingered, but could not last.
In every bloom, the shadows play,
Reminding us of love's decay.

Yet in decay, the seeds arise,
New life awakens, beneath the skies.
The cycle spins, and love endures,
Through the warmth of hope, our spirit cures.

So let us tend this sacred ground,
With tender hands, let love abound.
For in each rose, a truth is sown,
A path to grace, we walk alone.

Spirituality in a Surge of Sorrow

When sorrow crashes on the shore,
Our spirits tremble, evermore.
Yet in the waves, a lesson lies,
A chance to seek, to rise and rise.

The heartache sings a haunting tune,
Beneath the cold, the warming moon.
A sacred space where dreams collide,
In pain's embrace, our faith abides.

Each tear a prayer, each sigh a plea,
A journey through the depths to see.
Within the storm, the calm will grow,
As spirits dance in ebb and flow.

So let the sorrow swell and break,
For from the depths, new life we make.
In every surge, a light will gleam,
Awakening souls, igniting dreams.

In shadows cast, we gather strength,
To find our peace, no matter the length.
For in each sorrow, joy will bloom,
Revealing love, dispelling gloom.

Faith Amidst Fractured Whispers

In quiet corners, doubts entwine,
Fractured whispers, a heart's design.
Yet through the cracks, a light will beam,
Awakening souls from a broken dream.

With every word that wavers still,
A steadfast heart can bend, not kill.
In fractured notes, a song is spun,
Binding the lost, the weary, the won.

When shadows loom and futures seem gray,
Faith shines bright, and lights the way.
Through troubled waters, it will guide,
Embracing all, with arms open wide.

So gather close, the whispered choir,
As faith ignites a fervent fire.
Amidst the broken, love shall rise,
Transforming whispers into the skies.

For every whisper holds a prayer,
A sacred bond beyond compare.
In fractured faith, a strength refined,
Uniting hearts, our souls aligned.

Ceaseless Prayers for Healing

In shadows deep, we seek the light,
With hearts aglow, through darkest night.
Each whispered prayer, a sacred plea,
For grace to come, and set us free.

In stillness found, we lift our song,
In faith united, we grow strong.
The wounds of time, we bear with care,
In healing hands, our spirits share.

Through trials faced, we learn to stand,
Together bound, like grains of sand.
The warmth of hope, we hold so near,
In every breath, we cast out fear.

Divine embrace, our guiding force,
In every tear, we find our course.
Each moment steeped in love's pure grace,
Forever held in sweet embrace.

With hearts renewed, we rise again,
In ceaseless prayers, we find our zen.
The healing touch, a sacred art,
In unity, we mend the heart.

The Reverence of Departed Touch

In quiet hours, we feel their breath,
The memories bloom, beyond our death.
What once was lost, still lingers here,
A gentle whisper, forever near.

Through every prayer, their spirits rise,
A sacred bond that never dies.
In twilight's glow, we honor the past,
In every moment, their love amassed.

With every tear, a tribute made,
In loss we find, our souls are laid.
The touch of grace, a soft caress,
In reverence, we find our rest.

From shadows deep, their warmth unfolds,
In tender hearts, their stories told.
Each flicker shares a sacred vow,
In every loss, we honor now.

In sacred light, their presence shown,
The reverence of love, ever grown.
In quiet prayer, their spirits soar,
Forever cherished, we seek once more.

Light of the Wounded

In brokenness, we find our way,
The light within begins to sway.
Each fragile heart, though torn apart,
Holds radiant truth, a healing art.

The wounded soul, with shadows cast,
Hangs on to hope that holds us fast.
In darkest nights, we search for grace,
In gentle dawns, we find our place.

Through whispered dreams, we rise anew,
In every scar, the strength shines through.
The light of love, a guiding star,
Illuminates just who we are.

In trials faced, we dare to hope,
With wounded hearts, we learn to cope.
Each flicker bright, a beacon clear,
In light of love, we persevere.

Together bound, we stand as one,
In healing warmth, our fears undone.
The light we share, forever true,
In every heart, it starts anew.

Hymn of Broken Altars

Upon the stones where shadows lie,
We speak our truths, our spirits high.
In broken altars, we kneel and crave,
A sacred space, for hearts to save.

With every tear, a prayer is sown,
In silence kept, our grief is known.
The hymn we sing, in anguish deep,
A melody for souls that weep.

From ashes rise, a song of hope,
In brokenness, we learn to cope.
With trust in grace, we face the storm,
In love's embrace, our souls are warm.

In shadows cast, the light breaks through,
Reminding us of what is true.
In every trial, a lesson learned,
Through shattered dreams, our spirits yearned.

Together in our sacred space,
We find redemption, find our grace.
The hymn we share, our hearts entwined,
In every loss, new love we find.

The Commandments of Unfulfilled Love

In silence I call, your name on my lips,
A heart that is heavy, with torn, longing strips.
The first commandment echoes in darkness,
To love without limits, in soft, muted starkness.

Thou shall not forsake, the dreams we once spun,
In shadows of hopes, where our love was begun.
To cherish the whispers, that linger like smoke,
Though distance persists, and sweet vows we broke.

I bind my soul tight, still to the past,
Cling to the moments, too fleeting to last.
To forgive is divine, yet the pain dictates,
These commandments of love, that my heart so berates.

The weary soul wanders, down paths overgrown,
With echoes of laughter, that linger alone.
Thou shall not forget, the warmth of your gaze,
It's etched in my spirit, in a quiet haze.

Within sacred silence, I cradle my pain,
In the temple of memories, where joy turned to bane.
This love unfulfilled, stands resolute and stark,
Adorned in the shadows, forever its mark.

Love's Dark Procession

In the nightfall's embrace, our shadows collide,
With heartbeats entwined, where secrets abide.
Each step a reminder of what we once shared,
A haunting procession, of all that we bared.

Candles flicker low, the prayers barely said,
In the temple of sorrow, where echoes tread.
Thou shall hold the lantern, to guide me along,
Through valleys of heartache, where lost hopes belong.

The sky weeps for love, drowned deep in the sea,
A requiem sung, for what could never be.
With tears as my witness, I follow this path,
Each moment a chapter, that stirs up the wrath.

Cloaked in remembrance, I wander alone,
In love's dark procession, where hearts turn to stone.
The whispers of longing, cry out in despair,
While the spirit of love fades, beyond all repair.

But still I shall cherish, each shadowy trace,
For love's dark procession holds beauty and grace.
With every step taken, I honor the flame,
By holding your memory, my heart is aflame.

Anointing the Wounds of Love

In the quiet of night, my spirit does bleed,
With anointing of tears, my heart's sacred need.
Each tear a reminder of love's tender cost,
An altar erected for all that I've lost.

I wrap my sorrows in garments of grace,
With whispered confessions in this solemn space.
To heal the deep fractures, etched into my soul,
I tenderly nurture, the cracks that make whole.

Divine balm of patience, so gently applied,
Soothes the aching heart, where hope tried to hide.
Each wound tells a story, of passion and pain,
Anointed with love's gentle floods like the rain.

In the perfume of memories, I find my release,
Each moment recalled, brings a shadow of peace.
With hands stretched toward Heaven, I pray for repair,
To rise from the ashes, with love's gentle care.

For anointing the wounds is a sacred affair,
In the temple of longing, where hearts cease to bear.
With every soft whisper, my soul starts to mend,
And the wounds of our love, in triumph transcend.

The Joyful Agony of Remembrance

In the theater of dusk, where memories bloom,
I wander through echoes that lighten the gloom.
The joy and the agony, a delicate thread,
In the tapestry woven, of all that we said.

Like sunshine through leaves, your laughter does play,
An anthem of love, forever to stay.
Each moment we cherished, a treasure divine,
Yet shadows of longing, like wine intertwine.

I dance with regret, in steps of refrain,
For love's sweet remembrance holds both joy and pain.
In the swell of nostalgia, the heart learns to sing,
In the joyful agony, new hope takes wing.

The chapters we penned, still echo aloud,
Through the annals of time, where love feels so proud.
I honor the wounds, while I revel in light,
In the bittersweet union of day and of night.

For the joy of remembrance is sacred and true,
In the blissful agony, I carry in you.
Each heartbeat a testament of love ever bold,
In the dance of remembrance, our story unfolds.

Milton Keynes UK
Ingram Content Group UK Ltd.
UKHW021240191124
451300UK00007B/152